Garfield
hams it up

BY: JIM DAVIS

Ballantine Books • New York

Copyright © 1997 by PAWS, Incorporated.

All rights reserved under International and Pan-American Copyright
Conventions. Published in the United States by Ballantine Books, a
division of Random House, Inc., New York, and simultaneously in
Canada by Random House of Canada Limited, Toronto.

http://www.randomhouse.com

Library of Congress Catalog Card Number: 96-95038

ISBN: 0-345-41241-9

Manufactured in the United States of America

First Edition: March 1997

10 9 8 7 6 5 4 3 2 1

DEAR FLABBY

Snappy answers to sappy questions:
all your puny problems solved in 10 words or less!

Q: Dear Flabby,
What can I do about my little brother? He's such a pest!
A: Have you tried a flyswatter?

Q: Dear Flabby,
My boss is a mean, unappreciative slave driver who constantly belittles me. What can I do?
A: Shut up and get back to work!

Q: Dear Flabby,
My dad insists I clean my room! How can I get out of this?
A: Get a new dad.

Q: Dear Flabby,
Why are you so lazy?
A: Dear Loser,
Why are you so stupid? Next question.

Q: Help! I need to lose weight! How can I stop eating all the fattening foods I love?
A: Send them to me and I'll eat them for you.

OUT

in

THE NATIONAL CAT CHANNEL PRESENTS...

ED THE WONDER CAT, IN THE ACTION ADVENTURE...

"HAIRBALLS FROM OUTER SPACE!"

NOT EVERY CAT CAN WEAR TIGHTS

JIM DAVIS 3-13

THIS BOOK CONTAINS MANY GREAT INSIGHTS INTO LIFE

JIM DAVIS 3-14

AND WHEN YOU CONNECT THE DOTS, IT FORMS A PICTURE OF A BUNNY!

THAT WAS A TERRIBLE DATE

WE WENT TO THE CIRCUS

A CLOWN ACCUSED ME OF COPYING HIS SUIT

HOW LOW CAN A CLOWN STOOP?

JIM DAVIS 3-15

A LETTER FROM HOME!

YOUR FAMILY NEVER FORGETS

JIM DAVIS 3-16

"DEAR RON..."

OUCH

Dear Sir:
  On behalf of spider lovers everywhere, we wish to strongly protest your brutal treatment of our arachnid brothers and sisters.

Spiders are our friends. Spiders...

SMACK

UH-OH! HERE COMES THAT CAT! I'D BETTER PLAY POSSUM!

FLUSH

MUNCH
MUNCH
MUNCH

JIM DAVIS 4-21

URK!

COUGH COUGH COUGH HACK

HAACK

JIM DAVIS 5-12

ALL RIGHT! A COUPON!

WELL EXCUSE ME FOR BEING THRIFTY!

© 1996 PAWS, INC. Distributed by Universal Press Syndicate

CLONK!

I'M ATTRACTING A MORE SOPHISTICATED AUDIENCE

JIM DAVIS 6-10

THAT WAS AN ITALIAN SHOE

JIM DAVIS 6-11

GAR-FIELD!

MY GOOD SHEET!

NO MORE TOGA PARTIES

CLICK
CLICK
CLICK
CLICK
CLICK

HEY!

CLICK
CLICK
CLICK
CLICK

HE GETS MORE CHANNELS THAN WE DO!

CLICK
CLICK
CLICK

DON'T EAT THAT POOR, DEFENSELESS DOUGHNUT!

DON'T LISTEN TO HIM! CHOW DOWN, PAL!

DO WHAT IS RIGHT! DO WHAT'S IN YOUR HEART!

© 1996 PAWS, INC. Distributed by Universal Press Syndicate

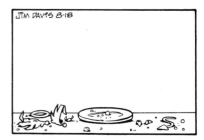

JIM DAVIS 8-18

SWAT

JIM DAVIS 9-11

HEY, CAT! I'M TALKIN' TO YOU!

JIM DAVIS 9-12

NOT SO HIGH AND MIGHTY WITHOUT YOUR NEWSPAPER, ARE YOU?!

WOULD YOU LIKE THE REST OF THIS SANDWICH?

THE CAPED AVENGER! FASTER THAN A SPEEDING DELIVERY TRUCK! TOUGHER THAN TAFFY!

ABLE TO EAT A LARGE PEPPERONI PIZZA IN A SINGLE BITE!

...WITH ANCHOVIES!

AHA! IT'S MY ARCHENEMY, THE INFAMOUS DOCTOR DWEEB!

UNHAND THAT CHEESEBURGER, OR RECEIVE A SEVERE THRASHING!

I HATE IT WHEN HE DOES THAT

ONCE, CATS WERE FEARLESS HUNTERS...

INDEPENDENT, STRONG AND PROUD

BUT, TODAY...

COULD YOU GET THE PLASTIC OFF THIS SLICE OF CHEESE?

JIM DAVIS 9-27

TODAY THEY ALL STARED INTO SPACE FOR A WHILE...

THEN THEY LICKED THEMSELVES AND TOOK NAPS

CAT NEWS

JIM DAVIS 9-28

I SAW THAT! GET UP HERE!

WHAT HAVE YOU GOT TO SAY FOR YOURSELF?!

Jim Davis 9-29

BURRRRRP

RUBY, THE DATING SERVICE SAID WE SHOULD GET TO KNOW EACH OTHER

JFM DAVYS 10-9

SO, EXACTLY WHY WERE YOU IN PRISON?

HIDE THE POTATO PEELER

OUCH

OK, RUBY, I'LL MEET YOU AT SEVEN

JFM DAVYS 10-10

BUT HOW WILL I KNOW YOU?

I SEE, THE TATTOO ON YOUR FOREHEAD READS "YBUR"

BUT, ARE THERE ANY DISTINGUISHING CHARACTERISTICS?

HAPPI-NESS IS...

SLEEPING THROUGH
A MONDAY

TRYING ALL
31 FLAVORS...
AT ONCE!

A 13 LB.
JELLY
DONUT

A PIZZA THE SIZE
OF SAUDI ARABIA

STRIPS, SPECIALS, OR BESTSELLING BOOKS . . .
GARFIELD'S ON EVERYONE'S MENU
Don't miss even one episode in the Tubby Tabby's hilarious series!

__GARFIELD AT LARGE (#1)   32013/$6.95
__GARFIELD GAINS WEIGHT (#2)   32008/$6.95
__GARFIELD BIGGER THAN LIFE (#3)   32007/$6.95
__GARFIELD WEIGHS IN (#4)   32010/$6.95
__GARFIELD TAKES THE CAKE (#5)   32009/$6.95
__GARFIELD EATS HIS HEART OUT (#6)   32018/$6.95
__GARFIELD SITS AROUND THE HOUSE (#7)   32011/$6.95
__GARFIELD TIPS THE SCALES (#8)   33580/$6.95
__GARFIELD LOSES HIS FEET (#9)   31805/$6.95
__GARFIELD MAKES IT BIG (#10)   31928/$6.95
__GARFIELD ROLLS ON (#11)   32634/$6.95
__GARFIELD OUT TO LUNCH (#12)   33118/$6.95
__GARFIELD FOOD FOR THOUGHT (#13)   34129/$6.95
__GARFIELD SWALLOWS HIS PRIDE (#14)   34725/$6.95
__GARFIELD WORLDWIDE (#15)   35158/$6.95
__GARFIELD ROUNDS OUT (#16)   35388/$6.95
__GARFIELD CHEWS THE FAT (#17)   35956/$6.95
__GARFIELD GOES TO WAIST (#18)   36430/$6.95
__GARFIELD HANGS OUT (#19)   36835/$6.95

__GARFIELD TAKES UP SPACE (#20)   37029/$6.95
__GARFIELD SAYS A MOUTHFUL (#21)   37368/$6.95
__GARFIELD BY THE POUND (#22)   37579/$6.95
__GARFIELD KEEPS HIS CHINS UP (#23)   37959/$6.95
__GARFIELD TAKES HIS LICKS (#24)   38170/$6.95
__GARFIELD HITS THE BIG TIME (#25)   38332/$6.95
__GARFIELD PULLS HIS WEIGHT (#26)   38666/$6.95
__GARFIELD DISHES IT OUT (#27)   39287/$6.95
__GARFIELD LIFE IN THE FAT LANE (#28)   39776/$6.95
__GARFIELD TONS OF FUN (#29)   40386/$6.95
__GARFIELD BIGGER AND BETTER (#30)   40770/$6.95
__GARFIELD HAMS IT UP (#31)   41241/$6.95

GARFIELD AT HIS SUNDAY BEST!
__GARFIELD TREASURY   32106/$11.95
__THE SECOND GARFIELD TREASURY   33276/$10.95
__THE THIRD GARFIELD TREASURY   32635/$11.00
__THE FOURTH GARFIELD TREASURY   34726/$10.95
__THE FIFTH GARFIELD TREASURY   36268/$12.00
__THE SIXTH GARFIELD TREASURY   37367/$10.95
__THE SEVENTH GARFIELD TREASURY   38427/$10.95
__THE EIGHTH GARFIELD TREASURY   39778/$12.00

Please send me the BALLANTINE BOOKS I have checked above. I am enclosing $_____. (Please add $2.00 for the first book and $.50 for each additional book for postage and handling and include the appropriate state sales tax.) Send check or money order (no cash or C.O.D.'s) to Ballantine Mail Sales Dept. TA, 400 Hahn Road, Westminster, MD 21157.

To order by phone, call 1-800-733-3000 and use your major credit card.

Prices and numbers are subject to change without notice. Valid in the U.S. only. All orders are subject to availability.

Name_____

Address_____

City_____ State_____ Zip_____

Allow at least 4 weeks for delivery   12/96

Like to get a **COOL CATalog** stuffed with great **GARFIELD** products? Then just write down the information below, stuff it in an envelope and mail it back to us...or you can fill in the card on our website - **HTTP://www.GARFIELD.com.** We'll get one out to you in two shakes of a cat's tail!

Name:
Address:
City:
State:
Zip:
Phone:
Date of Birth:
Sex:

Please mail your information to:

**Artistic Greetings
Dept. #02-7002
Elmira, NY 14925**

© PAWS